I Could Sing of Your Love Forever

Arrangements by: Mark Hayes, Kurt Kaiser, Lloyd Larson, Stephen Nielson, Jan Sanborn, Ovid Young

A FOREWORD . . .

Dear Keyboard Colleagues:

We are delighted to present to you "I Could Sing of Your Love Forever," Volume II in our collection of piano solo settings based on current worship materials. We've gathered together a stellar group of well-known and knowledgeable piano performers in the sacred arena, and they've created arrangements designed to be useful for you in worship services, in concert, for teaching purposes, or simply for your own worship experience.

We've chosen from quite a spectrum of worship music! Some of these titles will be familiar to you; others can be found for the first time in our "Seasons of Praise" collection (see back cover for more details). All of them will enlarge your own personal library, and provide variety for your performances.

As editor, I am grateful to Mark Hayes, Kurt Kaiser, Lloyd Larson, Steve Nielson, and Ovid Young for taking the time from their busy schedules to share their creative gifts with us. Special thanks goes to Dick Bolks for his consistently readable engraving. The process was most enjoyable.

Yours sincerely,

Jan Sanborn

Jan Sanborn
Keyboard Editor, Fred Bock Music Company

A TABLE OF CONTENTS . . .

I COULD SING OF YOUR LOVE FOREVER

MARTIN SMITH
Arranged by JAN SANBORN

17
21
25
29
33
mp

37
mf
41
f
45
49
53
sub. p

57
f
61
65
69
poco rall. e dim.
73
p a tempo
cresc. poco a poco

77
81
f
85
mp
rit.
89
p
r.h.

WE WILL GLORIFY

TWILA PARIS
Arranged by KURT KAISER

17
21
25
ten.
ten.
29
Legato
32
simile
p
mel.
mf

35
38
f
41
With conviction!
rall.
ff a tempo
44
48
mp

51
ten.
ten.
55
Freely
Ped.
59
Ped.
63
ppp

GREAT IS THE LORD

MICHAEL W. SMITH
and DEBORAH D. SMITH
Arranged by MARK HAYES

Moderately fast, with energy (𝅗𝅥 = ca. 76)

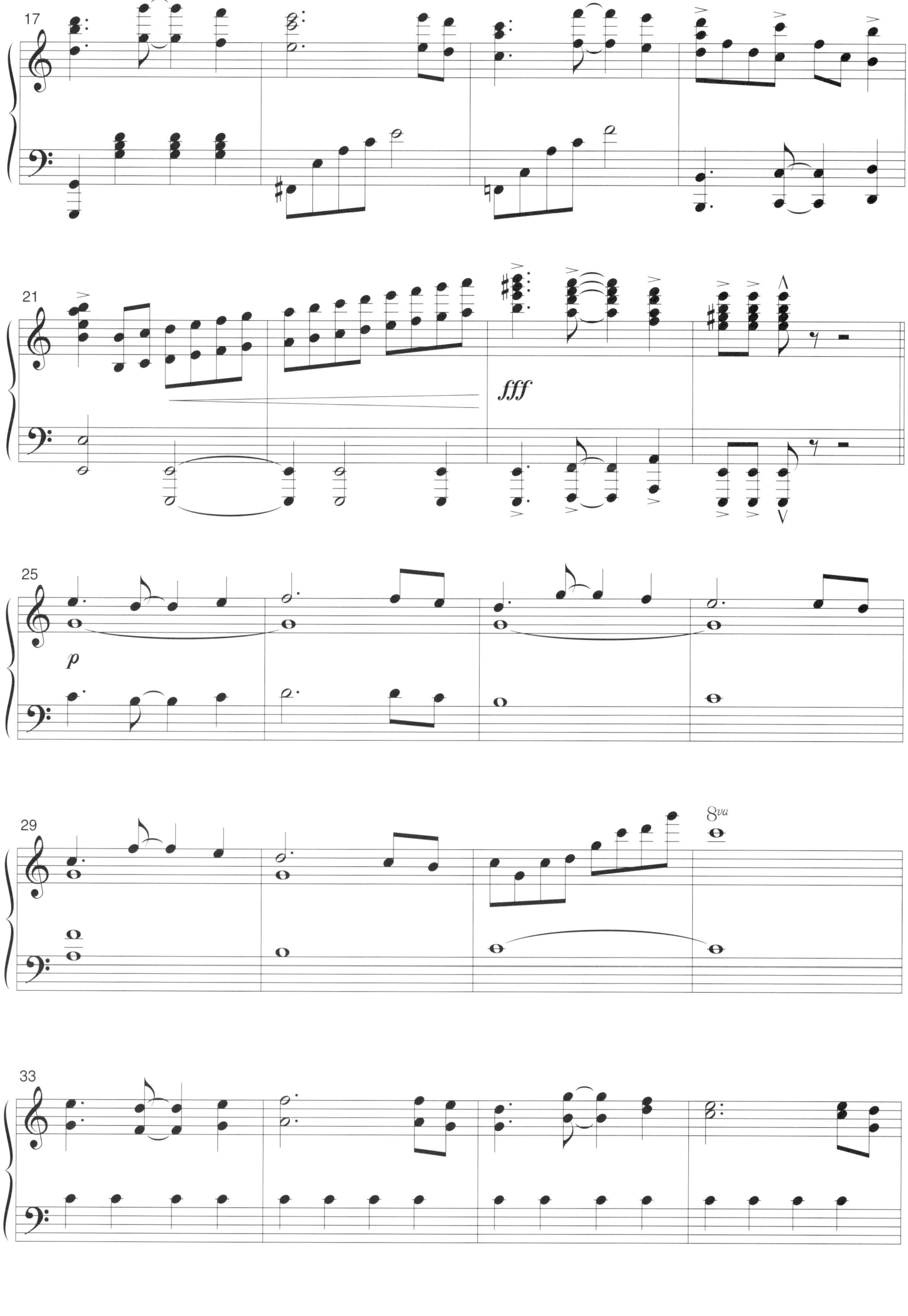
17
21
fff
25
p
29
8va
33

37
41
mf
8vb
45
(♮)
8vb
49
cresc. poco a poco
53
f

57
61
mp
65
69
3
mf
73

77
f
80
83
86
89

92
96
ff
p
100
cresc. poco a poco
103
3
molto rit.
ff
3
106
a tempo
fff

ALL WE DO

FRED BOCK
Arranged by OVID YOUNG

14
17
20
23
26
cresc. poco a poco

29
32
molto rall.
ff
34
mf
37
morendo mosso
poco rit. e dim.
41
p
l.h.
Ped.

EMMANUEL

BOB McGEE
Arranged by OVID YOUNG

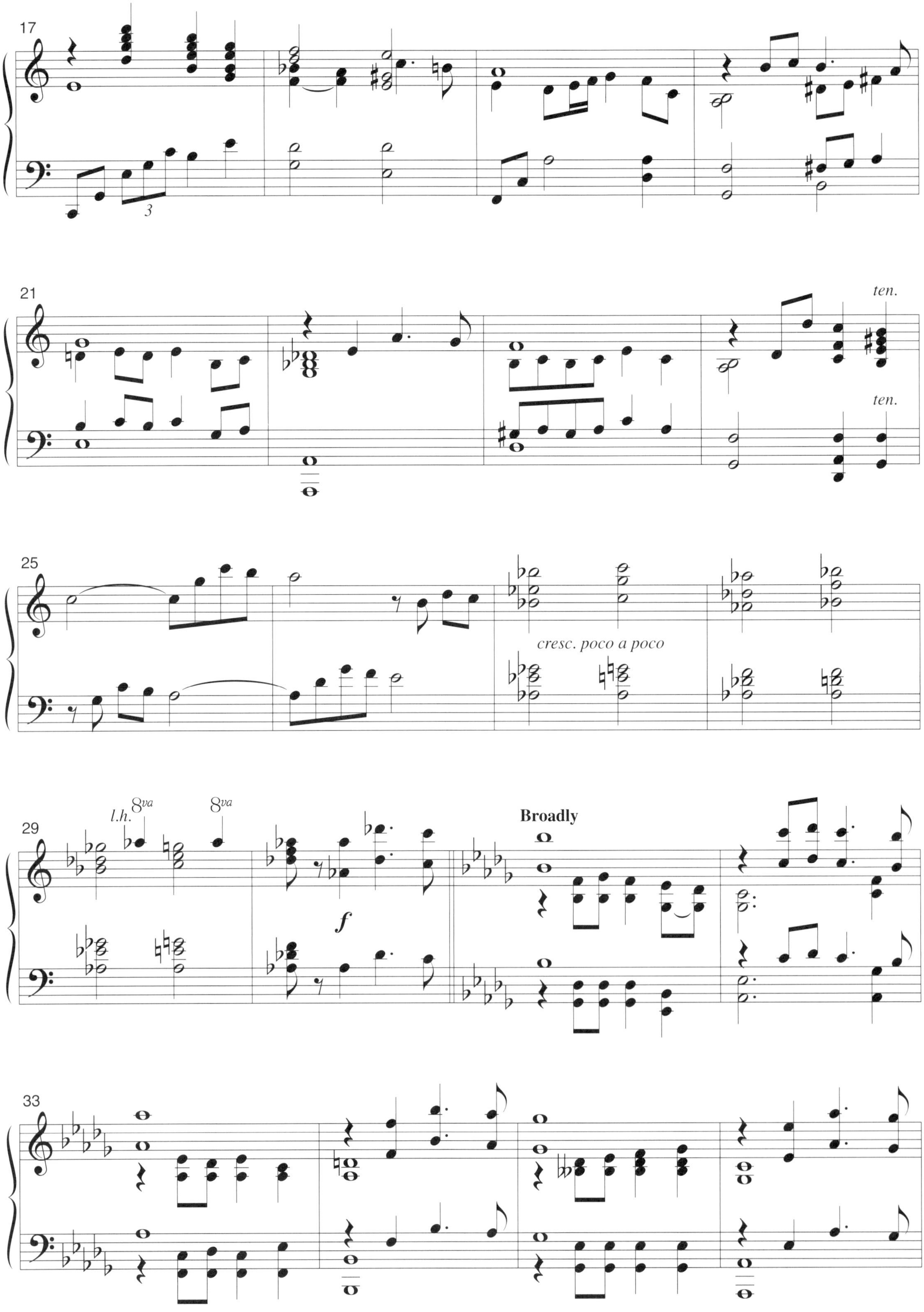
ten.
ten.
cresc. poco a poco
l.h.
8va
8va
f
Broadly

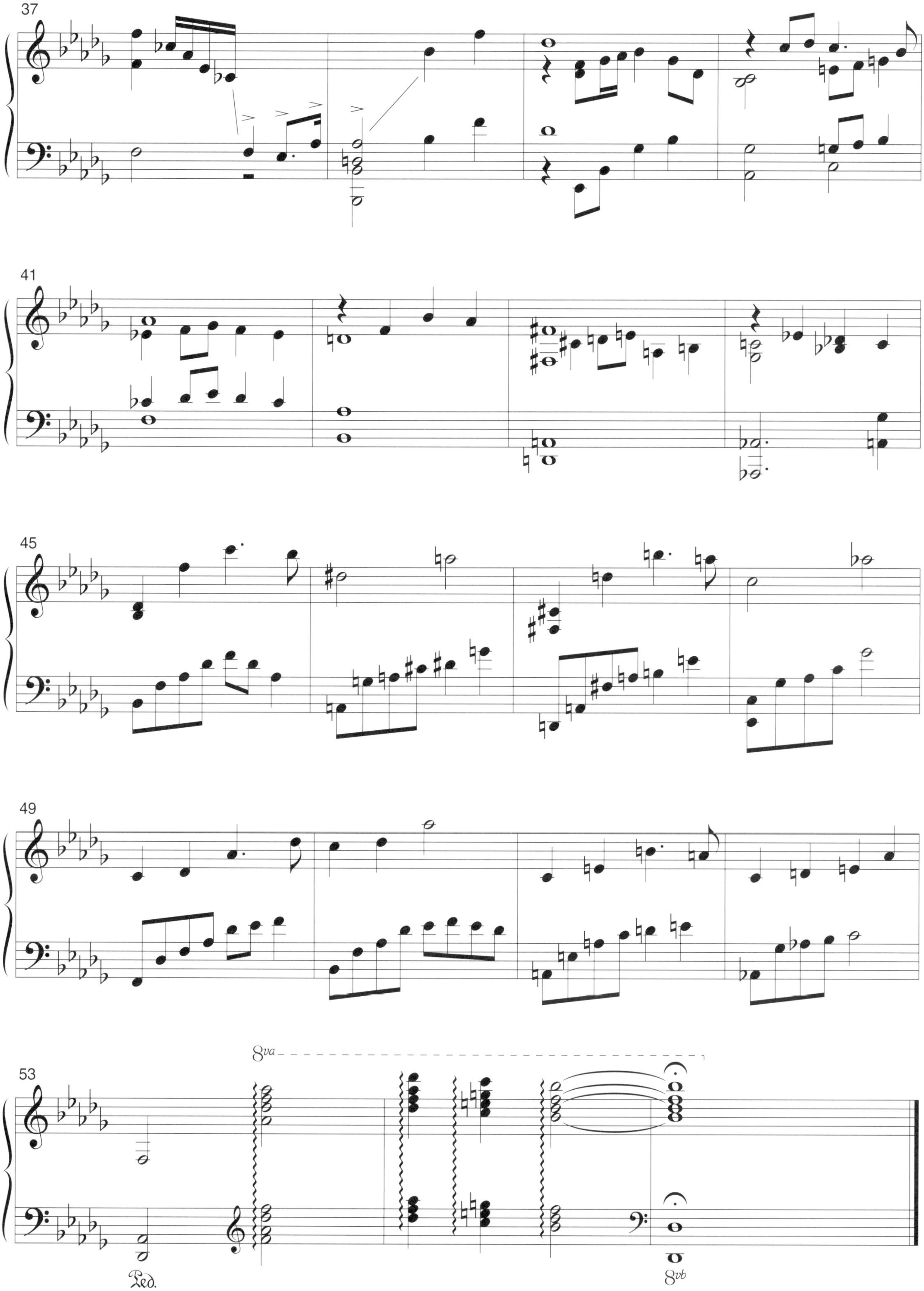
37
41
45
49
53
8va
Ped.
8vb

COME NOW, BEHOLD HIM

Music and Arrangement by
KURT KAISER

21
Variation II
f a tempo
25
29
rall.
Variation III
f a tempo
33
mp
mf
mp
37
41
Variation IV
p

45
49
Slower
Variation V
ff
53
57
dim.
Variation VI
mel.
mp
61
mf
65
mp
rit.
pp
Ped.
8vb

COME, SHARE THE LORD

BRYAN JEFFERY LEECH
Arranged by MARK HAYES

12
mf
15
mp
18
21
mf
24

Broadly, a little slower
27
ff
rit.
30
33
mf
36
rit.
mp
a tempo
rit.
39
a tempo
mf
rit.
mp

SAVIOR OF FALLEN HEARTS

DEBBIE SHAEFFER
Arranged by JAN SANBORN

17
21
mel.
25
mel.
mf
29
33
mp

37
41
45
mf
poco rall. e dim.
mp piu mosso
simile
49
53

57
cresc. poco a poco
61
f
65
dim. poco a poco
69
p
mf
73

77
mp
80
Ped.
83
rit. poco a poco
86
8vb

CHANGE MY HEART, O GOD

EDDIE ESPINOSA
Arranged by STEPHEN NIELSON

16
8va
ppp
3
3
mf
20
24
simile
28
molto cresc.
poco rit.
31
f a tempo
8vb

35
Largo (♩ = 63-66)
molto dim.
p dolce, molto espressivo
pp
39
43
poco rit.
46
8va
pp molto rit.
ppp molto morendo
Ped.
8vb

I GIVE YOU MY HEART

REUBEN MORGAN
Arranged by LLOYD LARSON

Gently, with a steady tempo (♩ = ca. 84-88)

13
16
mp
19
22
7
25
mf

28
31
mp
35
mf
38
41

44
47
50
3
f
53
56

59
ff
62
65
f
68
dim.
rit.
mp a tempo
71
dim. e rit.
p

TRUST IN THE LORD

Music and Arrangement by
LLOYD LARSON

13
16
mp
19
sub. f
22
25

28
mf
dim.
31
p
34
37
mp
cresc.
41
f

44
47
8va
mp
50
mf
f
54
57

61
64
ff
67
70
mf poco rit.
74
mp a tempo
8vb

COME, SEEK THE LORD

STEVE AMERSON
Arranged by STEPHEN NIELSON

With lyrical energy and simplicity (♩. = 60-64)

21
25
sempre staccato, leggiero
sub. pp
f a tempo
29
simile
33
ff
molto giusto
dim. e rit.
37
Flowing
mp a tempo

41
cresc. poco a poco
45
con forza
ff
49
molto leggiero
sub. pp
Cantabile
poco
rubato
mf
a tempo
mp
dim. poco a poco
53
poco
rubato
mp
a tempo
p
dim.
58
distant, delicatissimo
a tempo al fine
l.h.
mp
r.h.
8va
molto dim.
ppp
8vb